CONFLICTS AND CONFUSIONS

In Indian Culture

Swamini Vimalananda

First Published in June 2012 - 5000 Copies
Reprint February 2015 - 5000 Copies

Published by:
Chinmaya Prakashan
The Publications Division of
Central Chinmaya Mission Trust
Sandeepany Sadhanalaya
Saki Vihar Road, Powai, Mumbai 400072, India
Tel.: +91-22-2857 2367, 2857 5806 Fax: +91-22-2857 3065
Email: ccmtpublications@chinmayamission.com
Website: www.chinmayamission.com

Distribution Centre in USA:
Chinmaya Mission West
Publications Division
560 Bridgetown Pike, Langhorne, PA 19053, USA
Tel.: 1-888-CMW-READ, (215) 396-0390 Fax: (215) 396-9710
Email: publications@chinmayamission.org
Website: www.chinmayapublications.org

Illustrations: Anil Govalkar
Book Design: Radhika Chopra
Printed by: Parksons Graphics

Price: ₹ 160/-
ISBN: 978-81-7597-540-8

CONFLICTS AND CONFUSIONS
in Indian Culture

Swamini Vimalananda

Foreword

This book is dedicated to the great master,
Pūjya Gurudev Swami Chinmayanandaji whose life work and teachings will make every Indian and person of Indian origin proud of being the inheritor of a rich and enriching, as well as noble and ennobling culture.

The Indian scriptures say that the world is full of opposites. Our own experience too confirms that this world is indeed strange and contradictory. For every viewpoint there is a counter viewpoint and for every person that understands there are many more that do not understand and worst still, misunderstand.

Doubts and confusions arise because of incomplete knowledge or when there is conflict between two sources of knowledge; one could be our own mind. Indian scriptures therefore urge us to resolve all conflicts and confusions by learning from an authentic source and testing the knowledge with our own unbiased and complete thinking.

Indian philosophy and way of life (dharma) is followed by many even outside India. The glory of Indian thought and culture is that it has stood the test of time because of its capacity to adapt to changing times without losing its beauty, depth and meaning.

The resounding success of the book '*In Indian Culture – Why Do We*' made us realise that there is a huge demand to know about this fascinating land called India and its mind-boggling variety of beliefs and holistic lifestyle. Unfortunately it is understood by some, but misunderstood by many. This inspired the next book of the series on Indian Culture – *Conflicts and Confusions in Indian Culture* where certain fundamental and commonly misunderstood concepts of Indian beliefs and life-style are taken up. We urge the reader to read with an open and unbiased mind.

Contents

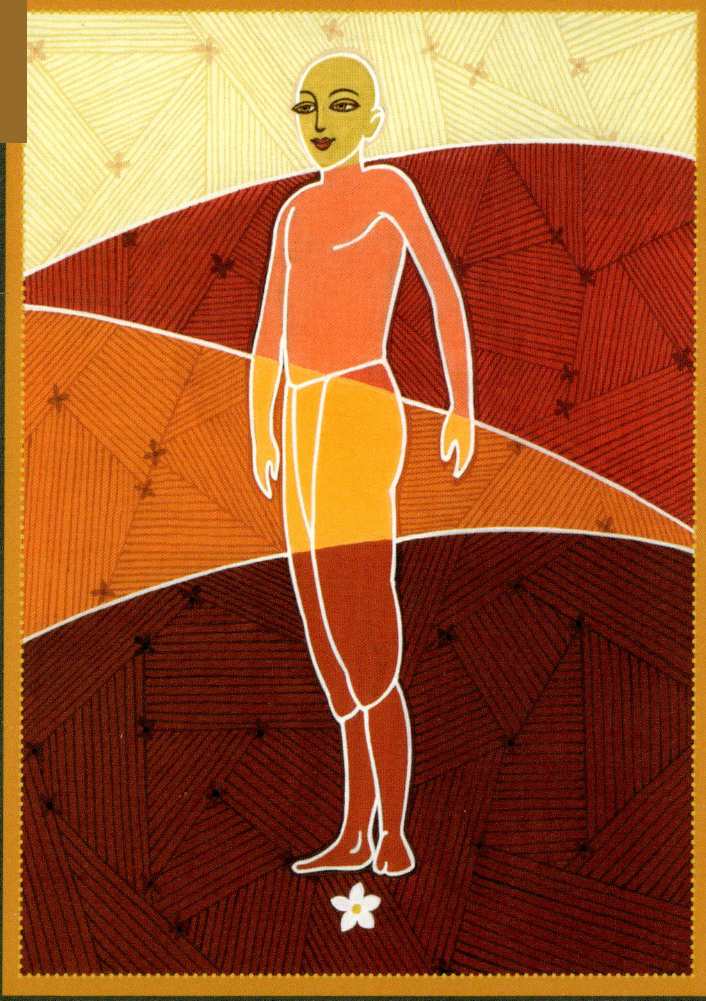

THE CASTE SYSTEM

Wherever there are human beings – in India as well as all over the world – there exists the 'varṇa vyavasthā'. Mistakenly called the 'caste system', which has created misunderstandings and negative connotations. Here, we will try and understand this universal system in more detail and with an open mind.

The word 'varṇa' means to describe. One describes an object by its qualities. Varṇa also means colour, hence the literal translation of varṇa vyavasthā is Colour System. Colour obviously does not mean the colour of the skin. Human beings are categorized into four types (varṇas) on the basis of their qualities (guṇas) and professions (karmas). This fourfold categorisation in India is called the Varṇa System.

The Three Guṇas

Everything in creation is made up of the three basic qualities (guṇas) – sattva, rajas and tamas which have the predominant characteristics of knowledge, activity and inertia respectively. Sattva includes faith, love, brilliance, understanding, remembrance, alertness, peace, compassion, sensitivity, selflessness and the like.

The quality of rajas embraces dynamism, ambition, restlessness, impatience, arrogance, doubt, anger, passion, confusion, greed and the like. Tamas includes carelessness, forgetfulness, sloppiness, sleepiness, dullness, wickedness, laziness and so on. It may be noted that tamo guṇa is opposed to both – rajas and sattva. For example laziness is opposed to action (rajas), forgetfulness to remembrance (sattva) and wickedness to goodness (sattva).

The Four Types of Human Beings

The fourfold categorisation of human beings on the basis of qualities (guṇas) is as below:

1. **Brāhmin:** Predominantly sattva (approx. 70%) backed by rajas (approx. 20%) and tamas (approx.10%).
2. **Kṣatriya:** Predominantly rajas (approx. 70%) backed by sattva (approx. 20%) and tamas (approx.10%).
3. **Vaiśya:** Predominantly rajas (approx. 70%) backed by tamas (approx. 20%) and sattva (approx.10%).
4. **Śūdra:** Predominantly tamas (approx. 70%) backed by rajas (approx. 20%) and sattva (approx.10%).

It should, of course, be understood that the proportions are approximate and not to be taken literally. They vary in different people but what is noteworthy is that all of us have each of the three qualities. No human being, however good or bad, can claim to have only one or two of the three. Also the proportion of these guṇas may vary in us at different times and stages in life. It is possible that a lethargic and laid-back person may, at a time in life, become dynamic and a go-getter. Ratnākara, a dacoit did become the famous composer of the Rāmāyaṇa, Sage Vālmīki. Such drastic changes are however not frequent.

Four Types of Professions

The three qualities prompt the four types of human beings into different professions:

1. **Brāhmins:** Being knowledge and peace oriented, they become teachers, researchers, priests, advisors, visionaries, artists and so on.
2. **Kṣatriyas:** Since they are action oriented and backed by noble intentions they become rulers, leaders, social workers, patrons of fine arts and so on.
3. **Vaiśyas:** Even though they are action oriented like the kṣatriyas, they are backed by profit motive and with an ability to mobilise and create wealth and resources. They, therefore, become traders, farmers, businessmen, entrepreneurs, moneylenders and so on.
4. **Śūdras:** Not being inclined towards knowledge or action, they are not self-motivated. They become good labourers, helpers, artisans, craftsmen, farmhands and so on.

When people take to professions (karmas) according to their qualities (guṇas) it is like fish taking to water. They have natural inclination towards their jobs and so love what they do. Hence, they grow, prosper and become happy. If however, the guṇas and karmas do not complement each other, there is a lot of hypocrisy, tension and frustration within, confusion and chaos in the field of action and suffering for all. A businessman who lawfully makes huge profits is admired, respected and awarded. On the other hand, a politician who works only for huge profits is condemned and disrespected. Mahatma Gandhi had a mass following, was feared by the British and is admired by the world, even though he had no money, power, arms or ammunition.

Many mismatches are evident in society. Rulers with faulty, selfish, or narrow visions have led their country to doom. In contrast, imaginative and bold leaders like Lee Kuan Yew of Singapore brought prosperity to his nation. Śrī Rāma's rule Rāma Rājya is considered an ideal as people of all the four varṇas did what they should be doing according to their guṇas, and thus all were happy and prosperous. Śrī Rāma (kṣatriya) ruled by the advice of Sage Vaśiṣṭha (brāhmin). There are some professions that require the characteristics of two varṇas. For example, the Vāstu Sāstra (Indian scripture on architecture) specifies that an architect must have the characteristics of both a brāhmin and a kṣatriya (designing, planning and execution). All the four varṇas are required for any system to function efficiently and successfully. It operates at all levels - individual, family, organisational, business, society and country.

If a family has only money-spinners and none to sweep the

home, it will be in a rich mess! At times, when it is found that the employees lack motivation, or the company needs direction, management gurus, motivators, inspirers (brāhmins) are invited. Some specialists provide vision statements or mantras. Saudi Arabia has the largest oil reserves but sought its much lacked protection from the US while America itself imported a labour force from the African continent.

A Universal System

Thus, seen with clarity, this system is universal and cannot be rejected. Taking the example of our own body, the head is the brāhmin (brāhmaṇaḥ asya mukham āsīt), the main organs of perception (seeing, hearing, tasting, touch, smelling) and thinking (brain) are located in the head. The head perceives, thinks, decides and guides. The arms and hands are the kṣatriya (bāhū-rājanyaḥ kṛtaḥ). They defend, attack and execute the work as planned by the head. The stomach is the vaiśya (ūrū tadasya yad vaiśyaḥ). It digests, dispatches, assimilates, stores and grows with the food it gets. The legs and feet are the śūdra (padbhyāṁ śūdraḥ ajāyata). They carry the weight of the body and transport the person wherever he desires to go. The mantras quoted are from the Puruṣa Sūktam of the Ṛg Veda, the oldest known book and scripture in the world.

In the body, the various parts work tirelessly throughout one's life for its welfare. If one part malfunctions, the entire body feels unwell. Each has its own special place of importance and hence there is no admixture of duties or rules. The feet do not protest about being always burdened and the mind about having to decide. A man may stand on his head for a few minutes, but will not be able to function well in that condition. However it is seen that whenever anybody is attacked, be it an Indian, American or African, the hands first protect the head.

Not only do we find these four categories in our body, but we even find these in the body cells too. We have the thinking (brain) cells that know and store information, the antibodies that fight and die to protect us, the fat cells that gather as much as possible and the carrier cells that work tirelessly transporting nutrients and removing wastes from various parts of the body.

Even though the Varṇa System is based on the qualities and profession, birth or heredity does have a role to play. It is observed that a child born in a family of musicians does have a natural flair for music or at least an ear for music.

Varṇa System in India

For those familiar with India and Indians, the following exercise will be interesting. Let us visualize the map of India right from Kashmir to Kanyakumari, Gujarat to Assam. The Kashmiri puṇḍitas are famous for their scholarship and the well-read libraries of Kashmir were full of the greatest philosophic literature. Punjab and Haryana has predominantly kṣatriya (Sardars, Jats) and vaiśyas. A number of men from these states join the defence services and the Green Revolution occurred in these states due to their action oriented temperament. Rajasthan has a predominantly kṣatriya (Rajputs) and vaiśya (Marwaris) and Gujarat has, predominantly, a vaiśya population. The Rajputs were famous warriors (Maharana Pratap); Marwaris, Sindhis and Gujaratis are renowned all over the world for their business acumen and generation of wealth (Mittals, Ambanis, Birlas). One would rarely hear of a Gujarati or a Sindhi in the defence services. Coming to the South, Tamil Brahmins form the majority of Indian scientists even at NASA. Thus, it is evident that all four varṇas have their own special place of importance in the system and there is no superiority or inferiority in terms of their work. Together, they all add and contribute to the uniqueness and beauty of India.

To conclude, the Varṇa System is a universal system of categorisation of human beings according to their qualities (guṇas) and professions (karmas). When people of all four varṇas work for the common goal, all prosper. When a man chooses his karma according to his guṇas he unfolds spiritually, feels fulfilled mentally and prospers materially. In short he is happy and successful.

....

THE UNTOUCHABLES

The mind thinks in terms of opposites. The concepts of clean and pure are also related to their opposites – dirty and impure. After a shower you feel clean and fresh and you keep away from dirt. Similarly when the mind feels peaceful, elevated or inspired or when goodness prevails within, you avoid contact with gossip, useless chatter or evil thoughts and people. You are thus practising untouchability at the physical, mental and social level. To keep away from or segregate yourself is your way of protecting yourself from the unwanted.

A Censurable Practice

However, to consider oneself superior to another on the basis of caste, creed, colour, profession, economic condition, religion, nationality and so on leads to hatred, prejudicial behaviour, suppressing and exploiting others and in extreme cases destroying them. An example is ethnic cleansing in Bosnia. Politics, laws and customs and segregation based on feelings of superiority cause suffering to all. The people of South Africa were segregated by the whites as Asians, Blacks and coloureds and they were grossly mistreated during the Apartheid rule. The native Indians were confined to reservations and the blacks enslaved without voting rights in the US and the Jews exterminated in Nazi Germany, all due to such false notions.

Untouchables in India

In India there exists Varṇa Vyavasthā, (wrongly called the Caste System) wherein people were categorized as brāhmins (thinking class), kṣatriyas (warriors, rulers, administrators), vaiśyas (farmers, traders and businessmen) and śūdras (labourers, artisans, craftsmen and helpers). This division was based on qualities (guṇas) and profession (karma) (Ref. 'Caste System'). Those who do not belong to these four either by guṇa or by karma were called outcastes or cāṇḍālas or antyaja. For example, people who lived a criminal life could fall into this category and were physically and socially segregated by the rest. They become the untouchables.

Every system is prone to its misuse. The four varṇas, especially the brāhmins, considering themselves superior, not only to the outcastes, but even to others, especially the śūdras (labourers, tribals, helpers, artisan, craftsmen and so on) created laws, customs and traditions which perpetuated mistreatment and unjustified behaviour. The śūdras and outcastes had no access to education, could not use the common water resources or road, and participate in religious rites and so on. Those who defied these taboos were severely punished.

Fortunately with time and education, this feeling of superiority based on varṇa is not seen much, at least in the big cities. However such feelings exist and are expressed even now in the villages of India. Politicians too, play varṇa politics and governments make varṇa based reservation policies, further segregating the society.

One may ask, is not segregation and avoiding contact in order to protect oneself also an expression of superiority stemming from a 'holier than thou' attitude? Yes, in many cases it may be so, but not always. The mature mind, even though remains non-judgmental towards others, knows what is good for oneself. Others may eat chocolates, but they are best avoided by me, if I am diabetic. A teetotaller would rather not attend a party if social drinking is mandatory in it.

In conclusion, the world over, 'untouchability' is practiced by many of us as a protection against the unwanted and by many stemming from a feeling of superiority which causes suffering to all.

....

THE DOWRY SYSTEM

The Indian marriage ceremony is a holy sacrament that unites a boy and girl in a lifelong relationship for fulfilling the four human goals of artha (security), kāma (desire or pleasure), dharma (doing righteous deeds and attaining inner unfoldment) and mokṣa (liberation). Keeping in view the four goals of life, wealth and the fulfilment of passion are not the only criteria for marriage.

The Highest Gift

The giving away of a daughter in marriage by her father (kanyā-dāna) is considered the highest gift that can be offered to the groom. The girl's parents give great attention to the choice of the groom for he must be worthy of their precious and beloved daughter.

The greatest gift is one which is given without expectation of anything in return. Hence the best marriages are those that take place without the exchange of gifts on either side. (Ref, 'Arranged Marriage System') The only gift is that of the daughter to her groom.

In olden days in India and also in some other contemporary societies, it has been customary for the boy's family to offer money or cattle to the girl's parents at the time of the marriage. Sometimes the girl's side laid down conditions before agreeing to a marriage. For example, in the Mahābhārata, Matsyagandhā's father sought assurance that her son alone would become king in place of Bhīṣma, the rightful heir to the throne. Such a conditional offering of a bride was not considered as the highest form of kanyā-dāna.

You can become a 'giver' only when the second party accepts your gift. The Hindus consider even the receiver of gifts worthy of respect and honour. So whenever a gift (dāna) is accepted by a person, he or she, in return, offers a dakṣiṇā as a token of gratitude. Formerly, money was in the form of gold coins and the dakṣiṇā usually comprised of one gold coin. This offering from the groom's side was referred to as 'vara-dakṣiṇā'.

The Girl's Gifts

The showering of gifts on the girl by her parents and others in the family is an expression of love. These gifts are called 'strī-dhana' – the woman's wealth. Traditionally, this was a voluntary offering according to the will and wish of the parents with no compulsions of any kind. Earlier, since wealth was in the form of land and property and could not be distributed to the daughter as she went to another village, giving gifts to her was a method by which parents ensured that she received a share of their assets.

The Wrong Practice

Everything changes and even the best of systems and attitudes get destroyed or perverted with time. 'Vara-dakṣiṇā' and 'strī-dhana' unfortunately degenerated into the very censurable dowry system. In that context, the groom's side sets a price and demands money, gold and property to be given along with the bride. Sometimes, the demands do not stop with the marriage ceremony, but continue for years after. The helpless bride's parents give away their life's earnings and get into lifelong debts to fulfill the unreasonable and unrighteous demands of the son-in-law and his family. They are compelled to do so out of fear for the girl's physical and mental well-being. This system of demanding goes against the very noble spirit of kanyā-dāna – the gift of a bride who is considered as Lakṣmī, the goddess of prosperity.

In conclusion, dowry system as is seen now is censurable and never formed part of the sacredness of Indian marriage values. It is the perverted form of vara-dakṣiṇā' and 'strī-dhana'.

....

THE ARRANGED MARRIAGE SYSTEM

In India, marriage is a union between not just two human beings but two families and communities. The marriage ceremony is an important sacrament by which the couple enters a very important stage of life called the gṛahasthāśrama, the householder life. This period is the foundation of family life devoted to upholding the lineage and its culture. The household forms the bedrock of society.

Types of Marriages

The Indian scriptures enumerate eight types of marriages, beginning with the lowest kind of marriage.

1. Paiśāca: The girl was abducted without her consent or the permission of her parents.
2. Rākṣasa: The girl was abducted without the parents' permission, but with her consent.
3. Āsura: The girl was given away for money.
4. Gāndharva: The girl and the boy fall in love and marry without the parents' permission.

In the above mentioned four cases, the marriage ceremony as prescribed by the scriptures was not performed. It is often performed later on for social acceptance.

5. Daiva: The father got the girl married to a man (sometimes a noble person) for the good deeds he had done.

6. Ārṣa: The father gave the girl in marriage and the boy's side gave wealth in return.

7. Prājāpatya: The father gave his daughter in marriage but under certain conditions. For example, in the Mahābhārata, Matsyagandhā's father stipulated that her son would be declared the heir to the throne in place of Bhīṣma, the eldest son and rightful heir.

8. Brāhma: The father gave the girl in marriage with no conditions and there was no exchange of wealth. Any gifts given were purely voluntary. This was considered the best.

Arranged Marriage

It is considered the dharma (duty), privilege and pride of the father to give his most precious daughter to the groom as kanyā-dāna, his gift. This was considered very meritorious. In choosing the groom importance is given to his family background, character, aptitude, age, health and looks. In contemporary times, the consent of the girl too, is sought before any decision is taken. Often the girl and boy make such a decision based on the aforementioned criteria. Such a choice is, therefore, not merely based on physical attraction or emotional involvement. It is a carefully considered decision with the recognition that the fulfilment of passion is not the main purpose of marriage. It is understood that there is nothing called a 'perfect match' and that true love is 'in spite of' and not 'because of' any factor.

As the couple live together they grow to love and understand each other. They adjust to each other's nature and commit themselves to caring for each other, the family and the wider community. This system proves sorrowful in instances when it is forced upon a couple and when the deciding factors for the marriage are wealth and status or when the demands for dowry are accepted. These factors are contrary to the spirit of the traditional arranged marriage system.

In conclusion, both love marriages and arranged mariages are acceptable according to the Indian scriptures. In an ideal marriage there is a strong physical, emotional, intellectual and spiritual bond. Such mutual love was expected to expand and include the family, relations and society.

....

ONE GOD, MANY GODS?

Only among Hindus do we find ignorance and confusion about a basic question like, 'Do Hindus believe in one God or many gods?'

One God

God is one alone, without a second. In His absolute nature He is nameless (anāma), formless (nirākāra), attributeless (nirguṇa), Existence-Consciousness-Bliss (Sat-Cit-Ānanda), the very Self (Ātmā) of all beings and therefore indicated as the Supreme Self (Paramātmā). He is called Truth or Reality (Brahman) in philosophy and the Lord (Īśvara) in religion.

As the Lord (Īśvara), He is omniscient (sarvajña), omnipotent (sarva-śaktimān) and omnipresent (sarva-vyāpi). He alone is the Creator (Brahmā) Sustainer (Viṣṇu) and Destroyer (Śiva) of the universe. He is both the material (upādāna) and sentient (nimitta) cause of the universe. In His mere presence and from Himself, His infinite power (māyā) creates the universe. He is therefore all-names (sarva-nāma), all-forms (sarvākāra) and all-qualities (sarva-guṇa). He alone expresses as life (jīvanam), life-giver (jīvana-dātā) and living beings (jīvas). He presides over all actions of all beings (karma-adhyakṣa) and gives results according to the actions (karma-phala-dātā). He alone incarnates (avatāra) as Śrī Kṛṣṇa or Śrī Rāma and assumes forms like Durgā, Lakṣmī, Gaṇeśa, Śiva and so on.

Some religions believe that God is formless (Islam), with form (Zoroastrian), in heaven (Christianity) and within us (Jainism). The Hindus believe He is both with and without form, farther than the farthest yet nearer than the nearest, both transcendental and immanent, both within and without.

Many Forms

Why does He assume so many forms? Would it not be easier if He had only one form?

Each of us has different likes, dislikes and inclinations. To cater to our particular demands, the Lord assumes various forms. Some find solace in worshipping the Lord as the Universal Mother (Ambikā) and some as an ideal, perfect and divine human being (Śrī Rāma). Generally speaking choice is a sign of progress, but poses a problem to the immature.

As I worship one form, what should be my attitude towards others? Do I have to worship all forms? (The altar in most Hindu homes is a museum of various forms of God and hence the confusion). We could choose one form that we like the best (iṣṭa deva). It helps concentrate the mind. Yet we should know well that He alone is all forms. For example, if Śrī Kṛṣṇa is our chosen form, we should consider Śrī Rāma and Śiva and all others as Śrī Kṛṣṇa's forms alone. So we may worship many forms or any form with the understanding that we are worshipping Him alone (sarva deva namaskāraḥ keśavaṁ pratigacchati).

The Hindus believe that in whatever form (even formless), in whatever way (chanting the name, rituals, meditation), with whatever attitude (selfish, noble), with whatever desire (for wealth, removal of sorrow, pleasures, heaven or liberation) we worship the Lord, He responds accordingly. (ye yathā māṁ prapadyante taṁstathaiva bhajāmyaham – Gītā 4.11)

Devatās (Deities)

There are innumerable actions that keep the universe going. Each of the functions or departments like rain, air, sun, water, and fire is headed by a functional or departmental head called adhiṣṭhāna devatā or simply devatā. For example, Indra, the presiding deity of heaven, is in charge of rain, Vāyu of air, Candramā (moon) of the mind and Agni of fire, speech and digestion. The relation between the mind and the moon is well established. Mental hospitals are called lunatic asylums, and a mental patient, a lunatic. People suffering from psychosomatic diseases are seen to be affected by the waxing and waning of the moon and madness increases during the new moon.

The Hindu scriptures speak of 33 crore devatās or deities or demigods. These deities are appointed by the supreme Lord and endowed with special, but limited powers to oversee the smooth functioning of their department. Those who worship the deities will obtain whatever they are capable of giving.

In conclusion, God is One. Even though He is formless in His true nature, He can and does assume many forms. He alone functions through the deities that overlook the functioning of the universe. One can worship Him in any form or every form.

....

IDOL WORSHIP

A common allegation made against the Hindus is that they are idol worshippers. Are Hindus idol worshippers?

The Ideal and the Idol

No, Hindus do not worship idols. They worship the ideal (God) represented by the idol. The Śiva-liṅga is the symbol (liṅga) of Śiva. When I salute the flag of my country, do I salute a stick and cloth or the ideals of my country represented by the stick and the cloth?

The Christians pray before the cross and the statues of Mary and Jesus, the Muslims turn towards the Kābā, the Sikhs worship the Guru Grantha Sāhib - their holy book, and the Zoroastrians worship fire. Are they all idol worshippers? All flags have symbolic meanings. Similarly all forms of God have symbolic meanings. For example the conch, disc, mace and lotus in the hands of Viṣṇu represent the four goals of dharma, wealth, pleasure and liberation that the Lord bestows on His devotees.

God is infinite and formless in His true nature. He manifests as the whole creation (all forms), incarnates in special forms (Śrī Rāma, Śrī Kṛṣṇa) and assumes many more forms (Durgā, Śiva, Gaṇeśa). He can therefore be invoked in any external form – stone, wood, tree, fire, sun, idol, picture, or within us as the divine Self.

Why do we need idols?

Why worship God in idols? Some keep the photograph of their beloved son in various stages of his life, in different rooms at home and even on their office table. The photograph reminds them of him, evokes love and gives solace in moments of loneliness. Even when one kisses the glass photo-frame, one feels one is kissing the child.

Similarly the idol, picture or symbol of the Lord reminds the devotee of His qualities and sports, elevates his mind and fills him with devotion. The idol provides the focus by which the devotee can direct his prayers and worship, express his feelings and feel His presence.

Is God in idols?

God is everywhere. Of course He is in the idol but not just only in the idol. He cannot be limited, for He is omnipresent. The devotee initially invokes His presence in the idol. With regular worship his mind gets uplifted and he is able to see

Him everywhere. Saint Ekanātha was carrying the holy Ganga water from Prayāga in North India to worship Lord Rameshwar in a temple in South India. Seeing the Lord in a thirsty donkey he gave away the precious water to him. A Śiva-liṅga is said to have appeared at that spot.

How is God worshipped through idols?

In India a guest is honoured and considered as God and God is worshipped in an idol as an honoured and revered guest. The altar is decorated beautifully, He is invoked in the idol, His feet are washed, He is offered sandal paste, holy rice, flowers, food, incense, ārati (vesper light)... - the best of all we have with a reverential and humble attitude. If a person feeds a stray dog daily he starts loving it. Will devotion not arise if we feed God with love and reverence?

In conclusion, Hindus are not idol worshippers. The idol represents the ideal (God) to be worshipped. Thus the infinite and all-pervading God can also be worshipped in the idol with offerings.

....

MANY SCRIPTURES, MANY WAYS, MANY MASTERS?

The Hindus have hundreds of scriptures and thousands of Masters, teaching a hundred different ways to reach the highest goal. To the uninitiated, it appears like a big Indian bazaar where hundreds are selling their wares – each extolling theirs as the best. So what is Hindu Dharma? What does it mean to be a Hindu? Which scripture describes it? Which is the best way? And who is the best amongst the Masters?

This confusion did not exist before, even though we have always had many scriptures, paths and Masters. In the school (Gurukula) the Master (Guru) taught the basic scriptures (Vedas) whereby the student got a complete grounding in Dharma and the essence of all scriptures and the path to be followed. Even when this system of education was replaced by the British system, the children got the basic knowledge of Dharma from pāṭhaśālās (Sunday schools), parents, the family priest and the family Guru. But today when the majority of Hindus do not practice their Dharma, when they have forgotten family traditions, when priests and Gurus are no longer honoured, it is little wonder that many people born in a Hindu family feel completely confused and lost.

Many Scriptures

A scripture (śāstra) is defined as that which gives complete knowledge of all aspects of a topic and frees us from all limitations. The Vedas are the basic scriptures of the Hindus. They are eternal truths revealed as mantras to Seers (ṛṣis) in their seat of meditation. These truths cover all aspects about the individual (jīva), the world one experiences (jagat) and their Creator (Īśvara). This vast body of knowledge was compiled into four volumes (Ṛg Veda, Yajur Veda, Sāma Veda and Atharva Veda) by Veda Vyāsa. The Vedas talk about how to live a good life here and hereafter (Dharma jñāna) and finally how to get liberated from the here and hereafter (Brahma jñāna).

The other basic scriptures are the various smṛtis (Gītā, Manu Smṛti...), the two Itihāsas (Rāmāyaṇa and Mahābhārata) and the eighteen Purāṇas (Śiva Purāṇa, Bhāgavata Purāṇa...). These were composed by great Sages and Seers, to explain the same Truth more elaborately. Various instructions on right living, techniques of spiritual practices, stories and examples of historic characters and incarnations of God, symbolism and so on are given in detail in these scriptures.

Various aspects of this knowledge were further talked about in aphoristic statements (sūtras), commentaries (bhāṣyas), poems (kāvyas), songs (bhajans), books of definitions (prakaraṇa granthas), sayings (subhāṣitas) and innumerable texts by various Saints, Sages and Masters over thousands of years. It is important to note that Hindus consider all knowledge and scriptures that reiterate the truths revealed in the Vedas as valid. Other texts of philosophy, however scholarly and popular they may be, are considered as invalid if they are not based on 'revealed knowledge' on the Absolute Truth.

The spiritual scriptures of India covered many topics like geography, history, sociology, geology, astronomy, geometry, astrology and so on. There are also great scriptures on non-spiritual subjects like medicine (Ayurveda), warfare (Dhanurveda), economics (Artha śāstra), politics (Nīti śāstra), architecture (Vāstu śāstra) and performing arts (Nāṭya śāstra) to name a few. These also spoke of ethical values related to that subject and the role of the subject in our spiritual evolution.

Many Ways

The goal of all human beings is to attain eternal and infinite happiness which is called Truth/Self in philosophy, and God in religion. Taking into account the different personality traits, Hindu/Sanātana Dharma expounds various paths and spiritual practices to reach God, and gives us the freedom to choose from them. The four main paths are briefly indicated below:

Path	Personality	Spiritual Practices
Jñāna Yoga - Path of Knowledge/ Enquiry	predominantly intellectual /contemplative	listening to the scripture (śravaṇa), independent reflection (manana) and contemplation/meditation (nididhyāsana)
Bhakti Yoga – Path of Devotion	predominantly emotional	repetition of God's name (japa), worship (pūjā), spiritual vows (vrata), pilgrimage (tīrtha yātrā) ...
Karma Yoga – Path of Action	predominantly action oriented, duty conscious	performance of duties (kartavya) or serving others (sevā) with the attitude of worship of God (arpaṇa buddhi), receiving results with the attitude of cheerful acceptance (prasāda buddhi)

Path	Personality	Spiritual Practices
Aṣṭāṅga Yoga – Path of Yoga	predominantly action and body oriented/ contemplative	Practice of virtues and disciplines (yama and niyama),postures (āsanas), breath control (prāṇāyāma), withdrawal of senses (pratyāhāra), concentration (dhāraṇa), meditation (dhyāna), absorption (samādhi).

Since none of us are exclusively intellectual, emotional or action oriented, the majority can follow a permutation and combination of spiritual practices best suited to our personalities and to the time, place and individual circumstances.

Many Masters

The Guru is one who removes ignorance by imparting knowledge. In the course of our life we have many Gurus starting with our parents, grandparents, teachers, friends, relations and colleagues. Nature and life's experiences have also taught us many things. In religious and spiritual matters too there are many Gurus. However the one who helps us determine the goal of our life and establishes us on the path to the Truth/God is called 'Sadguru'. He/she is the one to whom one turns to in doubt and distress, prays for guidance and worships at one's altar. One must have complete faith in his/her ability and nobility. Expert help in any field is essential to learn all aspects of a subject and to gain the required skill. Similarly, the Guru is the expert, the mentor, friend, philosopher and guide in life.

How does one find such a master in life? We need not search for a Guru. Our sincere demand for knowledge and guidance shall bring the right Master into our life. This is the experience of thousands of seekers. A Swami Vivekananda will eventually meet a Ramakrishna Paramahamsa.

In conclusion, 'Ekam sat viprā bahudhā vadanti' – 'Even though the Truth is one, it is spoken of in many ways in many scriptures by many Masters'. It is reached by many seekers in different ways guided by their chosen Masters. Our chosen spiritual practices and Master are best for us. When choice is a problem we can follow family traditions, sample a few, choose what best suits our personality and increase our sincere demand for the Truth.

....

LIFE, DEATH AND REBIRTH

What is life? What is birth and death? Why does one suffer while another experiences joy? Is this the only birth? These are some of the fundamental questions that every thinking individual seeks an answer to. There is much confusion, scepticism or disbelief even amongst practising Hindus.

Two bodies

Every individual has a gross body which is perceived, and a subtle body which cannot be perceived. The gross body is made up of the five gross elements (space, air, fire, water and earth), is born from the mother's womb and is the counter of all experiences of life. It grows, decays, and finally perishes at death. It is buried or burnt by others and returns to the elements of which it is composed.

The subtle body is made up of the five subtle elements. It consists of the five sense organs (ability to hear, feel, see, taste and smell), the five organs of action (ability to speak, grasp, move, excrete and procreate), the five physiological functions (breathing, excretion, circulation, ejection and digestion) and four-fold inner equipment (mind, intellect, memory and the I-notion or ego).

The Self

Within, yet beyond the two bodies, is the pure, infinite Self (Ātmā) which is neither born nor dies. It is also called Truth (Satyam), Reality (Brahman) or Consciousness (Caitanya) in philosophy and God (Īśvara) in religion.

What is life?

Life (jīvanam) is the manifestation of Consciousness/Self in the gross body through the medium of the subtle body. Let us take the analogy of a light bulb. The light (life) is the manifestation of electricity (Self) in the bulb (gross body) through the medium of the filament (subtle body). Whenever there is light (life) there must be electricity (Consciousness/Self). But wherever there is electricity (Consciousness/Self) there need not be light (life). The stone has Consciousness/Self/God, but no life, since it does not have a subtle body which alone can manifest life.

A being with a more developed subtle body is considered higher in the ladder of evolution. The amoeba is thus amongst the lowest of life forms and the human being amongst the highest.

What is born and what dies?

The body is ever changing and perishing. The Consciousness/ Self is unchanging and immortal. Connecting these two is the sentient ego, the individual which borrows its sentiency from the Self and identifies with the name, form and qualities of the two bodies. It owns the two bodies (I am fat, I am glad...), their actions (I sing, I think...) and the results reaped thereof (I enjoy, I suffer...). It goes through the three states of experience (I am awake, I dream and I sleep). It is this individuality alone that goes through the experience of birth and death (today is my birthday, I shall die one day...).

What is birth and death?

It is commonly accepted that the emergence of the child from the womb is its birth and that the ebbing away of life represents the death of a person. However in the light of what has been said earlier, birth is the entry of the subtle body into the gross body along with the individuality (jīva) that owns both. Some say that the individual enters at conception and some that it enters a few months later.

However it is commonly believed that the foetus in the womb is alive. Death is the departure of the individual from the gross body. The presence of the subtle body alone is the indicator of life in the body.

Is there rebirth?

The present birth of the individuality (jīva) is not its first. It has been going through innumerable lives (not necessarily human) from beginningless time and shall continue to do so, till it attains liberation (mokṣa). With so much of practice the individual has become adept at packing (of the subtle body at death) and moving from one house (gross body) to another, and then unpacking (of the subtle body at birth) in a new house (gross body). No part of the subtle body is ever left behind in the gross body. The dead man never sees or breathes!

Why does one suffer and another enjoy?

Even though all the gross and subtle bodies are made up of the same gross and subtle elements, there exists thousands of species and innumerable variety within each species. No two human beings look or think alike. Each one's experiences are different. What causes the difference?

As we sow so we reap. The gross and subtle body that one gets – the family, place of birth, life span, loss, gain, various circumstances and experiences of life are all the results of actions done in the past. Some actions give immediate results and others take months, years or even lifetimes to fructify. But whatever is done has to give results and the doer (jīva) alone becomes the enjoyer or sufferer of the results. That is the Law of Karma. As we enjoy or suffer the results of our actions, we create new karmas which get added to our karma account thereby continuing the cycle of birth and death.

Can a human being be reborn as an animal?

According to the scriptures there are 84 lakh species in creation. As per our fructifying karmas we can be born in any of these – plant, animal, human or any other. A person wears different clothes to suit the place and occasion. We choose to wear casual clothes for informal occassions and night dress for a comfortable sleep. Similarly the individual (jīva) takes on the gross and subtle body tailor-made to suit the fructifying results of his/her actions. For example, violent fructifying tendencies would get satisfied in a tiger's body, while blood sucking ones in the body of a leech. Or such tendencies could lead to a human birth and these and many more desires could be satisfied.

Basis of belief in rebirth

The majority of us do not know what happens after death nor do we remember what happened before birth. So what is the basis for our belief in rebirth or the reincarnation of the individual?

1. The Scriptures and Gurus

Scriptures like the Gītā, the Upaniṣads and the Rāmāyaṇa that talk about God, Truth and Dharma clearly state that the individual is reborn. For many people, faith in the scriptures and in the words of the Gurus is sufficient basis for belief in this concept.

2. Logic

The following logical fallacies occur if we do not accept rebirth:

• Fallacy of effect without a cause

There cannot be a result without an action. In this world we see some born poor, others rich, some are healthy, others unhealthy. There are child prodigies while others are born dullards. If birth is the absolute beginning then to what can one attribute such differences in people before they have even had time to perform any action? How does one logically explain a two year old child who has never heard the Gītā and yet is able to chant it faultlessly? The rememberer and the experiencer have to be the same. The child must have learnt it in a previous life.

• Fallacy of cause or action not producing effect or result

We see some individuals performing actions throughout their life, but do not see them getting all the results in their lifetime. What happens to them? Who reaps them? There has to be another birth in which the individual gets the results.

3. Experience

There are many known instances of people who remember their previous life in great detail during their first five years. The jātaka stories are the experiences of the Buddha's numerous previous lives. There are experiences of sceptics turned beleivers like Brian Weiss (author of Many Lives, Many Masters) and descriptions of people who had near death experiences (Life after Life by Raymond Moody) to show that the individual does not perish but survives death and reincarnates.

The concept of hell and heaven support the theory that the individual soul survives death and expereriences heaven or hell in some form. Early Christians, Buddhists, Jains, Sikhs and Hindus believe in the Law of Karma and reincarnation.

In conclusion, life is the manifestation of Consciousness/ Self/God in the gross body, through the medium of the subtle body. Birth is the entry of the subtle body along with the individuality into the gross body and death is its departure. As one sows, so one reaps here or hereafter. The individual who performs actions and reaps results when identified with the gross and subtle bodies, also transmigrates from one body to another till he/she attains liberation.

....

HEAVEN AND HELL

Is there a place called heaven or hell? Is our stay there eternal? Are they talked of simply to encourage us to do good and restrain us from doing evil? These are confusing concepts for many people.

Whether we believe in heaven or hell, what we all do understand is that heaven is bliss and hell is intense pain and sorrow. All of us have experienced intense joy and sorrow and have therefore sampled heaven and hell right here on earth.

Is there heaven and hell?

Every action gives its results. The good (puṇya) results in joy, the bad (pāpa) in sorrow. These results are enjoyed or suffered by the individual (jīva) at different times and places in different forms and bodies.

A place is designed to suit its purpose. A homely feeling or a work atmosphere is created by the site, structure, interiors, decor, the people and their feelings, attitudes and actions.

The place where we are born is also the result of our past actions. It is designed to best exhaust our fructifying karmas.

Some actions are ordinary, others extraordinay in their goodness or evil. The ordinary ones get exhausted in the various forms of earthly existence. The extraordinary, noble and divine ones result in heavenly joys, best experienced in heaven and demonic and evil ones in hell. Earthly limitations, the human body, earthly laws of diminishing returns and so on make it impossible to enjoy heavenly pleasures for long. Such pleasures are best enjoyed in heavely bodies in heaven. Consistent goodness or evil also results in heaven or hell.

Times of joy fly on wings and moments of sorrow seem to last forever. But heavenly joy or hellish sorrow even though long lasting by earthly standards, do eventually end. A man goes on vacation and enjoys himself till he runs out of cash and credit. He returns to sweat and toil to earn for his next vacation. In the same way, once our karmas are exhausted, we have to leave the place and the body and proceed to the next place in another body to reap the next set of fructifying karmas.

Is there eternal heaven or damnation?

Every action is finite and finite actions, however many in number, cannot yield infinite or eternal results. Therefore one cannot have eternal enjoyment or suffering in heaven or hell respectively. The scriptures describe various types of heavens and hells. This makes us aware of the results we shall face by our ordinary and extraordinay good and evil acts. A sensitive person does not need others to tell him to be good and the consequences of being evil. The joys and sorrows resulting from good and bad actions are expereienced by everyone in this world.

In conclusion, heaven and hell, like the earth, are planes of experiences which one reaps as a result of merits (puṇya) and demerits (pāpa) of a large number of consistent or extraordinary good or evil actions. Once the karmas are exhausted, the individual continues his journey to reap the next set of fructifying results in another place.

....

DESTINY AND SELF EFFORT

What is fate? Are some destined to fail despite their best efforts? Are some just plain lucky? Is God partial? Can we change our destiny? Are Hindus fatalistic?

What is destiny and self effort?

Every action must give its result. Cause precedes effect. The action done in the present will always bear result in the future – be it near or distant. Therefore what we get in the present is always due to our recent or distant past actions. The result of action itself is variously called – karma phala, prārabdha, fate, destiny or luck. The action performed by the individual is called self effort or puruṣārtha.

Can we change our destiny?

Swami Chinmayananda says, 'What we get in life is our destiny. What we do with what we get is our self effort.' In the light of this, it is we who create our own destiny which we are fated to enjoy or suffer. Even though we have no freedom in what we get, we can choose what to do with what we get.

Having once done an action, we cannot undo it. Every effort at undoing is a new action which will produce its own result. One action does not cancel the result of another. If a person commits ten good acts and ten bad acts, he will reap the results of twenty acts. Even though the good act does not cancel the effect of the bad act, it helps to create a better future or destiny for the person. The good acts also give the strength needed to go through the results of the bad actions.

Will the past always weigh on us?

Before starting any task, we weigh all the pros and cons and assess our assets and liabilities. Before embarking on a journey we understand the challenges that we will have to face from the beginning to the end. Similarly, in life's journey we should face our negative prārabdha as challenges and the positive ones as blessings.

Role of God in karma

If I get results according to what I do, what is the role of God? The body by itself is inert matter incapable of any action. It is Consciousness/Self/God that enlivens it and empowers it to act. God also creates the world – the field – in which man sows the seeds of action and reaps the results. Both the actions and the results are created and governed by God-made laws. He is therefore karma-adhyakṣa (one who presides over actions) and karma-phaladātā (giver of results of actions). Nature's/

God's laws are neither partial nor prejudiced. They appear just and kind to some, and partial and harsh to others. The teacher gives marks according to what we have written in the test. The teacher also gives grace marks to the deserving, who, but for the 'grace' might have failed the test!

Are Hindus fatalistic?

Many blame the laws of karma for their fatalistic attitude. Some await the turn of destiny to progress and prosper. Some blame the star signs for their problems. Some accept abject situations as their lot and believe that they are doomed to fail or to remain mediocre.

In contrast, the scriptures and saints urge man to work hard and prosper, to face and overcome all obstacles in achieving one's desired goal. Hands symbolise self effort. Each morning the Hindu looks at his hands and prays, 'Wealth, Knowledge and Divinity reside in my hand. May I attain them through righteous efforts.' It is also said, 'My hands are indeed fortunate'– as I can please Him with my sincere efforts. (ayam me hasto bhagavān)

The right attitude in facing destiny and self effort

We are generally tense and anxious whilst doing actions and elated or dissatisfied, frustrated or dejected by the results. This takes away the joy in action. The attitude of Karma Yoga enables one to consistently experience joy in action. We should selflessly perform all actions dedicated to a noble cause or to God (Īśvara arpaṇa buddhi) and cheerfully receive all results – good or bad, as gifts from Him (prasāda buddhi). To quote Swami Chinmayananda, 'What we have is His gift to us. What we do with what we have is our gift to Him.' Such an attitude keeps man motivated and inspired in action, yet fulfilled and content with the results.

In conclusion, what we get as a result of our actions is our destiny and what we do with what we get is our self effort. Destiny is thus the challenge we face in life's journey. The right attitude in doing actions and facing results makes this journey enjoyable and fulfilling. Therefore we should do our best and leave the rest to Him, whose just and kind laws govern all actions and results.

Transliteration and Pronounciation Guide

अ	a	fun	ट	ṭa	touch
आ	ā	car	ठ	ṭha	ant-hill
इ	i	pin	ड	ḍa	duck
ई	ī	feet	ढ	ḍha	godhood
उ	u	put	ण	ṇa	thunder
ऊ	ū	pool	त	ta	(close to) think
ऋ	ṛ	rig	थ	tha	(close to)pathetic
ॠ	ṝ	(long ṛ)	द	da	(close to) father
ऌ	ḷ	(long ṛ)	ध	dha	(close to)breathe hard
ए	e	play	न	na	numb
ऐ	ai	high	प	pa	purse
ओ	o	over	फ	pha	sapphire
औ	au	cow	ब	ba	but
अं	aṁ	**	भ	bha	abhor
अ:	aḥ	***	म	ma	mother
क	ka	kind	य	ya	young
ख	kha	blockhead	र	ra	run
ग	ga	gate	ल	la	luck
घ	gha	log-hut	व	va	virtue
ङ	ṅa	sing	श	śa	shove
च	ca	chunk	ष	ṣa	bushel
छ	cha	match	स	sa	sir
ज	ja	jug	ह	ha	house
झ	jha	hedgehog	ळ	(Note 1)	(close to) world
ञ	ña	bunch	क्ष	kṣa	worksheet
त्र	tra	three	ज्ञ	jña	*
ऽ	'	unpronounced अ (a)	ऽऽ	''	unpronounced आ (ā)

Note 1 : "l" itself is sometime used.
** Nasalisation of the preceding vowel.
* No English Equivalent
*** Aspiration of preceding vowel

NOTES